Inklings
of
Grace

Inklings
of
Grace

TERRY ALLEN MOE

Photographs by Dennis Dahlberg

Judson Press® Valley Forge

INKLINGS OF GRACE

Unless otherwise indicated, the Scripture quotations in this publication
are from the Revised Standard Version of the Bible copyrighted
1946, 1952 © 1971, 1973 by the Division of Christian Education
of the National Council of the Churches of Christ in the U.S.A.,
and used by permission.

Library of Congress Cataloging in Publication Data

Moe, Terry Allen.
  Inklings of grace.

    1. Meditations. I. Title.
BV4832.2.M55   242   81-13673
ISBN 0-8170-0941-8   AACR2

The name JUDSON PRESS is registered as a trademark
in the U.S. Patent Office. Printed in the U.S.A. ⊕

Gracious Inklings

Our lives are immersed in dimensions unseen and unfathomable. What we experience points beyond itself in inklings of the gracious Presence. Not only in, with, and under, but also before and after each moment, life's meaning stretches beyond measured event.

In these meditations I hope to point to the inklings of God's grace in our experience with other people and our encounter with the world. I have placed first the descriptions of experience, then passages from Scripture that address the episode, and finally a brief prayer. I have done this not to downplay Scripture and prayer by placing them later in the writings, but rather to emphasize the holiness of our experience as it is given by the Holy One.

The inklings are exactly that. Beginnings. Hints. Probings. Wonderings. My prayer is that these might touch off inklings of your own—and that they might be gracious ones.

Contents

1. Hearts and Faces: Inklings in Others

2. Inside Out: Inklings in Myself

3. Outside In: Inklings in the World

Part 1

Hearts and Faces: Inklings in Others

Ken: The Balloon Man

I didn't really know Ken until now. To be sure, we had talked—of life and job, of fishing and church. But I didn't really know Ken until he told me his name. Ken had once been active in the church—a leader of the men's fellowship and a member of the council. Who knows why he drifted away? Who could guess the causes? Who knows why anyone withdraws from others? Because of hurt or anger? Because one feels put down or not listened to? It could be any of a hundred reasons. For whatever reasons, Ken had become a recluse, seldom venturing from his tiny home where his television and newspaper provided his only company. The first few times I visited Ken I was frightened. His huge, podgy frame, balanced indelicately on red, scaly ankles, darkened the doorway of his dim hideaway. In the dank living room his eyes and nose and mouth seemed misplaced on his face, as if dislocated by his aloneness. But by now Ken's face and odor and walk were all familiar to me. Yet I didn't really know Ken until he told me his name.

The children of the block used to come to him to share the comic books that he stockpiled in his back room. Week by week they would read and reread the spongy pages in Ken's presence. "They must have called you something, Ken. What did the children call you?" I asked. A smile as broad as eternity from lips tight with aloneness revealed the answer: "The balloon man." And reaching into his pocket he pulled out a five- or ten- or twenty-year-old balloon. "I still carry them around with me. I always used to have a balloon for the children. I used to take them to the children at church, too. I always had a balloon."

Years have passed since Ken delivered balloons into eager, waiting little hands, but his pocket still holds his treasure. The children are grown and gone, but Ken still fondly handles this precious merchandise. Ken's pocket searching resulted in a balloon bearing his identity, his life's meaning in giving. Where can Ken give his balloons now? Who will share with the balloon man?

We, too, are balloon men, reaching to share, bearing cherished gifts in deep, hurtfilled pockets, wondering who will accept our offering. We, too, are balloon men struggling to find meaning in a present often radically disjointed from our past. We, too, are balloon men needing most desperately to share.

What shall I render to the LORD
   for all his bounty to me?
I will lift up the cup of salvation
   and call on the name of the LORD,
I will pay my vows to the LORD
   in the presence of all his people.
I will offer to thee the sacrifice of thanksgiving
   and call on the name of the LORD.
                 —Psalm 116:12-14, 17

When they had heard the king they went their way; and lo, the star which they had seen in the East went before them, till it came to rest over the place where the child was. When they saw the star, they rejoiced exceedingly with great joy; and going into the house they saw the child with Mary his mother, and they fell down and worshiped him. Then, opening their treasures, they offered him gifts, gold and frankincense and myrrh (Matthew 2:9-11).

He looked up and saw the rich putting their gifts into the treasury; and he saw a poor widow put in two copper coins. And he said, "Truly I tell you, this poor widow has put in more than all of them; for they all contributed out of their abundance, but she out of her poverty put in all the living that she had" (Luke 21:1-4).

We are carrying balloons, Lord, and we need to give. Our hands reach hopefully into our pockets to share our soul's treasure. You accept our thanksgiving. Thank you. Amen.

Otto: Struggling to Believe

For ninety-nine years Otto struggled to believe. Water splashed on his weeks-old hair and the catechism racked his adolescent mind. Church bells chimed his happy union—and memorialized his death. For ninety-nine years Otto struggled to believe. Through five wars in which humans killed humans in inhuman ways he struggled to believe. Through depression and recession and downright famine he struggled to believe. Through economic exploitation and racial prejudice and political oppression he struggled to believe. Did he wonder what was up when the atomic bomb first dropped? He cared about mothers who took abortion too lightly. Did he wonder why people could land on the moon and still not feed people on earth? He cared that his family was provided for. Did he seek God in the depths of his being where God prunes in order to cause growth? He struggled to believe.

There is no belief without struggle, no faith without doubt, no love without suffering. Thomas the doubter and Peter the bold one both shuddered in the garden. Each needed Jesus' special care. Philip the slow one and John the beloved both misunderstood and questioned and only through Jesus' ministry could say, "I believe."

We stand with Otto in the struggle for belief. God grant that we may not accept our belief too lightly as those without conscience, that we may not confess too easily as those who really do not understand, that we may not give up the struggle as those whose belief is cheap. God grant that we may live the love toward which "I believe" calls us.

On that day, when evening had come, he said to them, "Let us go across to the other side." And leaving the crowd, they took him with them in the boat, just as he was. And other boats were with him. And a great storm of wind arose, and the waves beat into the boat, so that the boat was already filling. But he was in the stern, asleep on the cushion; and they woke him and said to him, "Teacher, do you not care if we perish?" And he awoke and rebuked the wind, and said to the sea, "Peace! Be still!" And the wind ceased, and there was a great calm. He said to them, "Why are you afraid? Have you no faith?" And they were filled with awe, and said to one another, "Who then is this, that even wind and sea obey him?" (Mark 4:35-41).

And Jesus went on with his disciples, to the villages of Caesarea Philippi; and on the way he asked his disciples, "Who do men say that I am?" And they told him, "John the Baptist; and others say, Elijah; and others one of the prophets." And he asked them, "But who do you say that I am?" Peter answered him, "You are the Christ." And he charged them to tell no one about him.

And he began to teach them that the Son of man must suffer many things, and be rejected by the elders and the chief priests and the scribes, and be killed, and after three days rise again. And he said this plainly. And Peter took him, and began to rebuke him. But turning and seeing his disciples, he rebuked Peter, and said, "Get behind me, Satan! For you are not on the side of God, but of men" (Mark 8:27-33).

I believe that I cannot by my own understanding or effort believe in Jesus Christ my Lord, or come to him; but the Holy Spirit has called me through the Gospel, enlightened me with his gifts, and sanctified and kept me in true faith (explanation of the Third Article of the Apostles' Creed, *Luther's Small Catechism*).

"I believe." What strong words! What a bold statement! Almost foolishness to utter them! You know my struggle to believe, God. Let me never give up. But more importantly, let me never forget that you are faithful, that you call me to believe, that it is from you that I receive the gift of belief. Amen.

Hermann: Cancer Call

I went to Hermann with ministry in mind—to speak a word of God's presence to his waning life. I went expecting to bring hope and expectation. I went fearfully and with a quivering heart. But Hermann ministered to me instead. He said, "On the road to Emmaus . . ."—and he pronounced "Emmaus" the German way and paused here and there to gather German thoughts into English sentences—". . . Jesus was present." What else could he say? The Word unfolded from a spirit unattacked by the cancer afflicting his body. The Word was clearer, even, as a result of the chaotic cell division within him.

God, you speak with human lips to me. I don't always hear; but when I do I never cease to be amazed, for your Word is so potent, so full of life, so irresistible! Thank you for letting me hear your Word in the betweenness of your Spirit. Thank you that somehow you minister in the betweenness of our relationships! To think that ministry is not something bought or sold, laid upon or conjured up, but is your Spirit working with us to recall your Word in power! Thank you for the gift of your Spirit in ministry.

"Behold, the days are coming," says the Lord GOD,
  "when I will send a famine on the land;
not a famine of bread, nor a thirst for water,
  but of hearing the words of the LORD.
They shall wander from sea to sea,
  and from north to east;

16

they shall run to and fro, to seek the word of the LORD,
but they shall not find it.

—Amos 8:11-12

Then he opened their minds to understand the scriptures, and said to them, "Thus it is written, that the Christ should suffer and on the third day rise from the dead, and that repentance and forgiveness of sins should be preached in his name to all nations, beginning from Jerusalem. You are witnesses of these things. And behold, I send the promise of my Father upon you; but stay in the city until you are clothed with power from on high" (Luke 24:45-49).

He said to them, "It is not for you to know times or seasons which the Father has fixed by his own authority. But you shall receive power when the Holy Spirit has come upon you; and you shall be my witnesses in Jerusalem and in all Judea and Samaria and to the end of the earth" (Acts 1:7-8).

Lord Jesus, open your Word to me in others. Let its meaning flow from life's exchanges, from chance meetings and organized agendas, from lifetime relationships and casual acquaintances, from quiet solitude and busy togetherness. Let your Spirit minister in our midst. Amen.

Berta: Blood and Roses

Berta gave the better part of her life to the blood bank: she solicited donors, drew blood, made sure that those in need would be supplied. Some friends called her "Blood-Bank Berta." But she had other names as well, for her hands were close to the dirt, almost a part of the earth. Her twinkling eyes blossomed with roses of every description from yard to anniversary bouquet to uniquely laced Christmas tree as she recalled her ministry of roses. And her heart enfolded the Bible, which she always spelled in capital letters, even as she spoke the word: "BIBLE!"

It was as though Berta pumped blood through the green earth, forcing up roses for human delight. Then *she* lay, huge hands gnarled with work, her own body in need of blood. And our hands seek to imitate Berta's, to follow our Creator's. We, too, push up roses of different dimensions, each a newness. The Word stands at our center as the organ that gives and receives life.

What kind of hands broke bread in an upper room? Were they hands roughened by earthly work? What blood flowed on a cross but blood for all in need? What heart ached with grief, spelling out the Bible's truth? What life brought roses to our hearts to share? Christ's blood pulsates deep in the earth of our being, pushing up roses from a perfect heart of love.

In the beginning was the Word, and the Word was with God, and the Word was God. He was in the beginning with God; all things were made through him, and without him was not anything made that was made. In him was life, and the life

was the light of men. The light shines in the darkness, and the darkness has not overcome it (John 1:1-5).

But when Christ appeared as a high priest of the good things that have come, then through the greater and more perfect tent (not made with hands, that is, not of this creation) he entered once for all into the Holy Place, taking not the blood of goats and calves but his own blood, thus securing an eternal redemption. For if the sprinkling of defiled persons with the blood of goats and bulls and with the ashes of a heifer sanctifies for the purification of the flesh, how much more shall the blood of Christ, who through the eternal Spirit offered himself without blemish to God, purify your conscience from dead works to serve the living God (Hebrews 9:11-14).

Our hands join Berta's in seeking roses. Our hearts unite with Berta's in seeking life. Our blood pours out a prayer for roses and hearts. Amen.

Rudy: Ja! Ja!

Rudy prayed in my presence "with sighs too deep for words" as he said, "Ja, ja." The first "ja" was higher toned and louder, while the second trailed off in the deeper intercession of life's breath. His "ja" was not the simple yes of stoic resignation, but the deeper yes of suffering involvement. He spoke of war: "Ja, ja." We talked of hunger: "Ja, ja." Of poverty: "Ja, ja." Of loneliness: "Ja, ja." Rudy's "Ja, ja" seemed to echo Jesus' "Thy will be done."

Rudy's prayer reflected not understanding, nor even acceptance, at least as one commonly understands it, but rather a recognition of participation—in war, in hunger and poverty, in loneliness—a kind of sigh of our humanness that transcends individual and nation and class and stature. Deep within Rudy is the ready prayer: "Ja, ja." He says, "I don't do much anymore. I'd like to, but I can't. When you get older, you just can't do things like you used to." And a pause. "Ja, ja." Old age and Rudy himself are added to his list of intercessions.

And they went to a place which was called Gethsemane; and he said to his disciples, "Sit here, while I pray." And he took with him Peter and James and John, and began to be greatly distressed and troubled. And he said to them, "My soul is very sorrowful, even to death; remain here, and watch." And going a little farther, he fell on the ground and prayed that, if it were possible, the hour might pass from him. And he said, "Abba, Father, all things are possible to thee; remove this cup from me; yet not what I will, but what thou wilt" (Mark 14:32-36).

We know that the whole creation has been groaning in travail together until now; and not only the creation, but we ourselves, who have the first fruits of the Spirit, groan inwardly as we wait for adoption as sons, the redemption of our bodies. For in his hope we were saved. Now hope that is seen is not hope. For who hopes for what he sees? But if we hope for what we do not see, we wait for it with patience.

Likewise the Spirit helps us in our weakness; for we do not know how to pray as we ought, but the Spirit himself intercedes for us with sighs too deep for words. And he who searches the hearts of men knows what is the mind of the Spirit, because the Spirit intercedes for the saints according to the will of God (Romans 8:22-27).

God, our sighs are deep within us. Our prayers are often unspoken. Still, it is you who prompts our deepest longings. It is you who prays for us, even as we pray to you. Rudy's prayer was "Ja, ja," and there is no other. Thy will be done. Amen.

Brad: The Truth Repeated

Brad looked in perplexity at the banner hanging from a rude post in the camp mess hall. This had been quite a week for Brad and for fourteen other mentally retarded teenagers who had shared a week of outdoor camping. He had swum in the pool where he contentedly paddled, endlessly entertaining himself by repeating his favorite words: "JOO-OO-OO—CE, JO-OO-OO—CE" or "FAAAAANS, FAAA—AANS." He had hiked and sung and played silly games only grumblingly—all the time repeating his favorite expressions as if new meaning were somehow added with each repetition. His counselor, Jim, had grown to love Brad. His repetitious mutterings, his peculiar preoccupations, his apparent detachment from others all endeared him in a peculiar way.

Now Brad stood before a banner as rudely constructed as the building that housed it. No longer was Brad a disabled child to be pitied or helped. Rather, as he stood before this banner, haltingly reading and rereading its lines, Brad was the very Word of God: "I a-a-am the wa-a-ay, the t-t-t. . . ." "*Truth*," added Jim, faced by truth. ". . . the t-t-truth, a-a-and the li-i-ife." And Brad's spontaneous smile encircled Jim in an embrace. The Word had spoken.

For five weeks Jim had walked in and out beside the words of the banner. But it took Brad to make them alive. For five weeks the words were present. But it took Brad to make them the Word of God to Jim. His stuttering statement lifted Jim in its arms and pointed him to its referent: Jesus. Letters of a book now took on flesh and blood in the communion of Brad and Jim in Jesus. As Jesus is the truth of God spoken in human form, so Brad humanly repeated God's truth. It took no supernatural knowledge, no miraculous cure of his disability, no seminary education—only prayerful repetitions, silly little games, and a rudely hung banner. Brad led Jim in the way.

"Let not your hearts be troubled: believe in God, believe also in me. In my Father's house are many rooms; if it were not so, would I have told you that I go to prepare a place for you? And when I go and prepare a place for you, I will come again and will take you to myself, that where I am you may be also. And you know the way where I am going." Thomas said to him, "Lord, we do not know where you are going; how can we know the way?" Jesus said to him, "I am the way, and the truth, and the life; no one comes to the Father, but by me. If you had known me, you would have known my Father also; henceforth you know him and have seen him" (John 14:1-7).

. . . Jesus answered, "You say that I am a king. For this I was born, and for this I have come into the world, to bear witness to the truth. Every one who is of the truth hears my voice." Pilate said to him, "What is truth?" (John 18:37-38).

Lord Jesus, you are the way: guide us.
Lord Jesus, you are the truth: fill us.
Lord Jesus, you are the life: bear fruit in us. Amen.

Jerry: Making Room at the Table

The young boy eagerly pushed his way to the Communion rail. It was as if the pulpit were an obstacle to be overcome as he squeezed between it and the woman next to him, leaving her husband standing until the next opportunity to kneel. Aggressively he half knelt, half leaned against the pulpit as if to say "You'll not exclude me here!" How anxiously he came to the throne of grace! How seriously he accepted God's blessing upon his head!

But this young boy knows disappointment. He's been squeezed from other tables, excluded from other communions, pushed from blessing and life. Grandpa and Grandma raise him as best they can. His father is in prison and his mother is who-knows-where.

This young boy reaches out to God in our midst. He seeks the communion of believers that is God's church. This young boy, eagerly pushing to cover the pain of past disappointment, is Christ among us—hungry, lonely, in prison. This young boy is the least of these—and the greatest.

The Spirit of the Lord GOD is upon me,
    because the LORD has anointed me
to bring good tidings to the afflicted;
    he has sent me to bind up the brokenhearted,
to proclaim liberty to the captives,
    and the opening of the prison to those who are bound;
to proclaim the year of the LORD's favor,
    and the day of vengeance of our God;
    to comfort all who mourn. . . .

—Isaiah 61:1-2

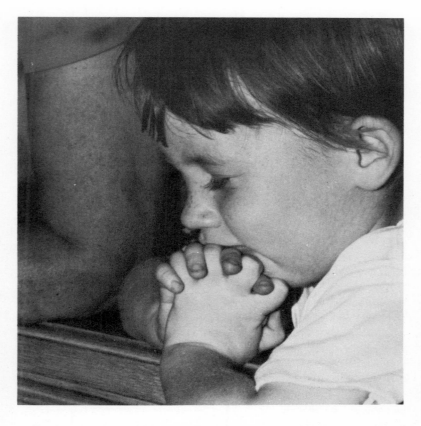

And he closed the book, and gave it back to the attendant, and sat down; and the eyes of all in the synagogue were fixed on him. And he began to say to them, "Today this scripture has been fulfilled in your hearing" (Luke 4:20-21).

"Blessed are the poor in spirit, for theirs is the kingdom of heaven.

"Blessed are those who mourn, for they shall be comforted.

"Blessed are the meek, for they shall inherit the earth" (Matthew 5:3-5).

We are grateful, God, for a place at your table. Help us to reach all of your children with your good news of a banquet hosted by your Son, Jesus Christ our Lord. Amen.

Elmer: Will You Join Our Circle?

Our Sunday Adult Forum was going quite well. We were chewing on the idea that God's grace and judgment are a single movement, two sides of the same experience. As we discussed, in walked Elmer. Who was this stranger from outside on the street? Who was this soft-spoken intruder who testified to personal pain and looked the part? Did he drift in from nowhere—a nobody carrying his heart on his sleeve? George slipped inconspicuously to the narthex and met Elmer. "Can I help you?" he asked. "Yes . . . yes, I think you can. I have quite a few personal problems. . . . I don't know. . . . I. . . ." Elmer nervously shuffled through the brochures and bulletins on the table. "Would you like to join our church school class? We just began our discussion," George invited. At first Elmer was reluctant. Strange people. A strange place. Would these people squeeze him into a mold? Would they force him into confession? Would they coerce conversion, pulling his heart from his breast? George reassured him, inviting him a second time: "We'll just pull up another chair. Will you join our circle?" So he did.

Elmer spoke of pain, nearing his threshold time and again, backing off, and then reapproaching it. His flannel shirt, coming untucked at the bottom, and the sawdust around his collar spoke of work. His broken teeth and cloudy eyes reflected hard experience. Who was this stranger in our midst? Did his soft-spoken expression hide a deeper pain? Were his eyes bloodshot from lack of sleep or alcohol?

I began to wonder if my shirt was tucked in. Did my soft-spokenness bury deeper pain? Were my eyes on the threshold of revelation, but reluctant to be opened? I began to see myself in

Elmer's agonizing question, which he threw before the group: "What does it mean to be saved?" His hard experience became mine. His broken heart, one we all shared. His experience of nobody/nowhere/nothing touched us with judgment and grace. George's invitation became God's: "Will you join our circle?"

Judgment and grace: together. The judgment: you are needy, your pain is great, your experience hard, your eyes hesitating, your circle far from full. The grace: God is with the needy, God shares your experience, God has overcome the world. As we touch our need, our pain, our hard experience, there is Christ. The grace/judgment: Christ.

The earth quakes before them,
 the heavens tremble.
The sun and the moon are darkened,
 and the stars withdraw their shining.
The LORD utters his voice
 before his army,
for his host is exceedingly great and very terrible;
 who can endure it?

"Yet even now," says the LORD,
 "return to me with all your heart,
with fasting, with weeping, and with mourning;
 and rend your hearts and not your garments."
Return to the LORD, your God,
 for he is gracious and merciful,
slow to anger, and abounding in steadfast love,
 and repents of evil.
—Joel 2:10-13

He said therefore to the multitudes that came out to be baptized by him, "You brood of vipers! Who warned you to flee from the wrath to come? Bear fruits that befit repentance, and do not begin to say to yourselves, 'We have Abraham as our father'; for I tell you, God is able from these stones to raise up children to Abraham. Even now the axe is laid to the root of the trees; every tree therefore that does not bear good fruit is cut down and thrown into the fire" (Luke 3:7-9).

"Nevertheless I tell you the truth: it is to your advantage that I go away, for if I do not go away, the Counselor will not come to you; but if I go, I will send him to you. And when he comes, he will convince the world concerning sin and righteousness and judgment: concerning sin, because they do not believe in me; concerning righteousness, because I go to the Father, and you will see me no more; concerning judgment, because the ruler of this world is judged" (John 16:7-11).

You are a consuming fire, O God, and a gently warming ember. You are a crushing hammer and a mighty shield. You are a plower, the sower of new seed, and the harvester of the crop. Thank you, God, that your judgment is righteous and that your grace is abundant. Help us to experience your love in grace/judgment. Amen.

Part 2

Inside Out:
Inklings in Myself

It Is Resurrection

Easter Sunday I returned from services carrying my special chalice wrapped carefully in a dish towel. I had brought the chalice from its safety to use on this special day. As I returned it to its safe shelf, I thought to myself, *What if it falls down and breaks?* I dismissed the thought by reassuring myself that since it had sat contentedly on the shelf for six months, there was no reason for it to fall now. Still I wondered.

Not even half an hour later I heard a crash in my office. I knew. Still I wondered. When I entered I saw that, sure enough, the chalice had fallen, shelf and all, and it now lay in pieces on the floor. How had it happened? An earthquake? A careless placement of the shelf and/or chalice? I'll never know. But I wonder.

I wonder what it means. The rough edges of my broken chalice cry out to me, but my ears are stopped. The abrupt decapitation of the graceful stem seems to point beyond itself. The smooth glaze interrupted by crude, unfinished clay proclaims its truth. What would you tell me, God? I wonder.

Shall I put you back together, chalice—the way you used to be? Would you ever be the same? In a way, though, I like you better broken because your brokenness better symbolizes life. The beauty and the symmetry remain but are broken to the core by accident, by deafness, by will, by wonder. The sturdy stem remains—decapitated hope and broken love—still strong. It is resurrection. The Spirit fills even brokenness.

God, you once were broken. You, too, stood tall and beautiful in symmetry but were shattered by a cross. The pieces remain. I clutch

31

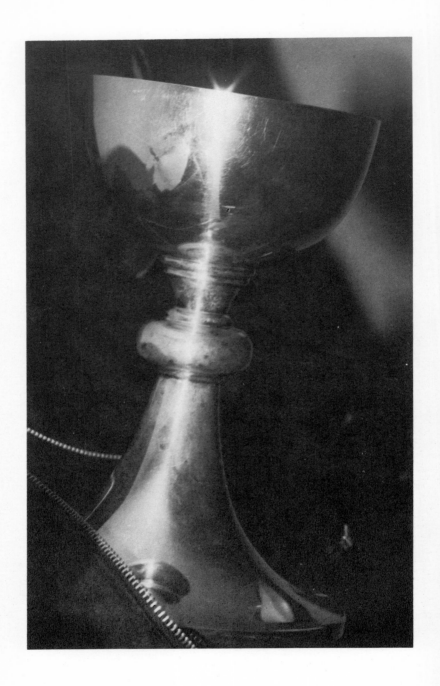

your broken pieces—and wonder what it means. Your divinity was interrupted by human cruelty killing hope and love on a cross. The pieces remain. But your brokenness heals ours. Your Spirit joins our pieces. It is resurrection. I clutch the pieces. It is resurrection.

But on the first day of the week, at early dawn, they went to the tomb, taking the spices which they had prepared. And they found the stone rolled away from the tomb, but when they went in they did not find the body. While they were perplexed about this, behold, two men stood by them in dazzling apparel; and as they were frightened and bowed their faces to the ground, the men said to them, "Why do you seek the living among the dead? Remember how he told you, while he was still in Galilee, that the Son of man must be delivered into the hands of sinful men, and be crucified, and on the third day rise." And they remembered his words, and returning from the tomb they told all this to the eleven and to all the rest. Now it was Mary Magdalene and Joanna and Mary the mother of James and the other women with them who told this to the apostles; but these words seemed to them an idle tale, and they did not believe them (Luke 24:1-11).

Have this mind among yourselves, which is yours in Christ Jesus, who, though he was in the form of God, did not count equality with God a thing to be grasped, but emptied himself, taking the form of a servant, being born in the likeness of men. And being found in human form he humbled himself and became obedient unto death, even death on a cross. Therefore God has highly exalted him and bestowed on him the name which is above every name, that at the name of Jesus every knee should bow, in heaven and on earth and under the earth, and every tongue confess that Jesus Christ is Lord, to the glory of God the Father (Philippians 2:5-11).

Jesus, we wonder at your resurrection. We wonder at our lives, both when we sense our wholeness and when we feel in pieces. We thank you that the wonder of your resurrection fills the wonder of our lives. Amen.

If Only Life Were Really like That

His favorite television show was "Grizzly Adams," about a man, a bear, and the mountains. As the concluding theme song faded, he looked at me with a sigh that came from deep within: "I wish life were really like that." But I knew the television's portrayal of life was unreal, just as the tubes and wires within the set were without life. Reality is not togetherness and peace nor simple resolutions nor painless gardens of pleasure. But I didn't need to tell him that. His sigh was a knowing sigh, a sigh holding his Vietnam War experiences, his loneliness, his disappointment in child rearing, his suffering— all in deep, prayerful words: "I wish life were really like that."

The words are history's prayer: for peace when history is bloodied by strife; for togetherness when time is marred by separations of race, nation, family, religion, and economics until only loneliness is left and even the individual is relentlessly divided within. It is humankind's prayer, its longing for good when evil presses in upon it. Fresh-baked bodies from Nazi ovens cry, "Why?" Parentless children with adult responsibilities wail, "I wish!" Psychoanalyzed introverts caught in the web of empiricism are squashed by their self-questionings: "I wish life were different." And all humanity lowers its head to this prayer.

Could this be Jesus' prayer as well? Could his painful garden have led him to longing? Could his "why hast thou forsaken me?" be his brutal questioning of cruel reality? Could his bloody crucifixion frame humanity's hellish existence within the arms of God's love? Could God's love be so foolish and so great?

Our God wishes with the pain of death another life for us and

unfolds upon that death the promise of a new reality. Our God responds to our longings. The bear and the child shall walk together. The lion and the lamb shall feed gently upon the grass. The waves will no longer rage nor the foundations quiver. The children will all belong—and God will be their home. The longing prayer of humankind will be answered. For great is our God in all the earth and greatly to be praised is God's name.

The wolf shall dwell with the lamb,
   and the leopard shall lie down with the kid,
and the calf and the lion and the fatling together,
   and a little child shall lead them.
The cow and the bear shall feed;
   their young shall lie down together;
   and the lion shall eat straw like the ox.
The sucking child shall play over the hole of the asp,
   and the weaned child shall put his hand on the adder's den.
They shall not hurt or destroy
   in all my holy mountain;
for the earth shall be full of the knowledge of the LORD
   as the waters cover the sea.

—Isaiah 11:6-9

Then I saw a new heaven and a new earth; for the first heaven and the first earth had passed away, and the sea was no more. And I saw the holy city, new Jerusalem, coming down out of heaven from God, prepared as a bride adorned for her husband; and I heard a loud voice from the throne saying, "Behold, the dwelling of God is with men. He will dwell with them, and they shall be his people, and God himself will be with them; he will wipe away every tear from their eyes, and death shall be no more, neither shall there be mourning nor crying nor pain any more, for the former things have passed away" (Revelation 21:1-4).

"I came that they may have life, and have it abundantly" (John 10:10*b*).

Good Shepherd, we have dreams—often painful dreams that border on unreality and wishful thinking. Help us to hold on to dreams. Help us to ground our wishful thinking in you. Guard us from self-delusion and withdrawal from the world. Lead us into life as you intended. Amen.

Remembering and Celebrating

For some, remembering is a painful burden they are reluctant to bear. For some, remembering is an unnecessary pastime, a useless exercise of fools and those who have no present for which to live. But for us as Christians, remembering is the essence of our lives. We are a remembering people. And for some, celebrating is the jovial postponement of today's problems and worries, a kind of respite from the world of care. For some, celebrating is an impossibility because they are so wrapped up in inducing pleasure artificially that the thought of real celebration eludes them. But for us as Christians, celebrating is the focus of our lives. We are a celebrating people.

We remember not hollowly as people with no hope. We remember boldly as those who truly belong. We remember deeply as those whose trust is beyond experience. We remember care-fully and pain-fully as those whose communion is grounded in suffering. We remember constantly as people whose eating and drinking are signs of God's presence.

We celebrate not shallowly as those whose celebrations fluctuate artificially with the whims of time. Rather, we celebrate the coming of light in the darkest hour. We celebrate the power of weakness itself, the resonance of a whispering wind, the quiet breath of the spirit. We celebrate not as those seeking inebriation from life while oblivious to its joys and sorrows, but as participants in the deepest levels of what is human, where joy and sorrow show God's oneness above them. We celebrate continually as those whose broken bread speaks sustenance and thanksgiving in the present.

But chiefly we are a remembering and celebrating people because we have a remembering and celebrating God: a God who in Christ has shared our joys and sorrows, our struggles and high points; a God who remembers and celebrates with us.

"Hear, O Israel: The LORD our God is one LORD; and you shall love the LORD your God with all your heart, and with all your soul, and with all your might. And these words which I command you this day shall be upon your heart; and you shall teach them diligently to your children, and shall talk of them when you sit in your house, and when you walk by the way, and when you lie down, and when you rise. And you shall bind them as a sign upon your hand, and they shall be as frontlets between your eyes. And you shall write them on the doorposts of your house and on your gates" (Deuteronomy 6:4-9).

And it was told King David, "The LORD has blessed the household of Obededom and all that belongs to him, because of the ark of God." So David went and brought up the ark of God from the house of Obededom to the city of David with rejoicing; and when those who bore the ark of the LORD had gone six paces, he sacrificed an ox and a fatling. And David danced before the LORD with all his might; and David was girded with a linen ephod. So David and all the house of Israel brought up the ark of the LORD with shouting, and with the sound of the horn (2 Samuel 6:12-15).

One of the criminals who were hanged railed at him, saying, "Are you not the Christ? Save yourself and us!" But the other rebuked him, saying, "Do you not fear God, since you are under the same sentence of condemnation? And we indeed justly; for we are receiving the due reward of our deeds; but this man has done nothing wrong." And he said, "Jesus, remember me when you come into your kingdom." And he said to him, "Truly, I say to you, today you will be with me in Paradise" (Luke 23:39-43).

Rejoice in the Lord always; again I will say, Rejoice. Let all men know your forbearance. The Lord is at hand. Have no anxiety about anything, but in everything by prayer and supplication with thanksgiving let your requests be made known

to God. And the peace of God, which passes all understanding, will keep your hearts and your minds in Christ Jesus (Philippians 4:4-7).

We give you thanks for the lives of those we remember. We praise you for those with whom we celebrate today. But chiefly we offer thanks for your Son, Jesus Christ our Lord, whom we remember and celebrate. Amen.

Door

Here is the door.
It stands so unpretentiously amidst a myriad of attractive alterna-
    tives.
THE DOOR.
    Who could know that God's mystery would be enclosed
    . . . in a human being!
THE DOOR.
It looks so plain. So much a part of the human fabric.
What is this DOOR? (And Pilate's question, "What is truth?" and
    countless,
    ageless questions sit patiently at this DOOR.)
A *human being?*
    HA!
    I need a door with pearly gates and St. Peter checking credentials!
    HA!
    I need a narrow way I can choose for myself, assuring direct
        access.
    HA!
    I'll do it my way! You can have your door. I'll have mine.
    We'll meet on the other side.
    HA!
    I want a door I can peep through before entering—just in case.
But a *human being?*
    Why, that's no door at all.
    More like an obstacle. . . .
I can't define this DOOR. Nor measure its dimensions. Nor push it
    open or shut.

This DOOR demands what it is—a *human being.*
Not my mind
> or my physical strength
>> or my personal piety
>>> or my offering and good works.

This DOOR demands me!
  I quiver before this DOOR.
This DOOR shatters my controlled life.
  I am showered with LIFE overflowing.
YOU, DOOR, are not what I expected.
YOU, DOOR, deepen the mystery.
YOU, DOOR, invite me in.

"Truly, truly, I say to you, he who does not enter the sheepfold by the door but climbs in by another way, that man is a thief and a robber; but he who enters by the door is the shepherd of the sheep. To him the gatekeeper opens; the sheep hear his voice, and he calls his own sheep by name and leads them out. When he has brought out all his own, he goes before them, and the sheep follow him, for they know his voice. A stranger they will not follow, but they will flee from him, for they do not know the voice of strangers." This figure Jesus used with them, but they did not understand what he was saying to them. So Jesus again said to them, "Truly, truly, I say to you, I am the door of the sheep. All who came before me are thieves and robbers; but the sheep did not heed them. I am the door; if any one enters by me, he will be saved, and will go in and out and find pasture. The thief comes only to steal and kill and destroy; I came that they may have life, and have it abundantly" (John 10:1-10).

There are many doors, Lord. You stand at each one, offering life. Guide me through the doors of my life. When I shudder before necessary doors, strengthen me; when I falter through foreign doors, forgive me; when I wander into unknown doors, enliven me to faith in you. Amen.

What's It Like?

Twelve-year-old Scott wouldn't celebrate New Year's Day this year. His friend of eleven years—his cat, Tooter—had died that morning. He showed me a picture of Tooter he had drawn. All I could see were thick table legs until he pointed Tooter out: "That's Tooter, there. She liked to rub the table legs." We shared a few minutes of memories about Tooter, and then I asked how he felt. "Does it feel like a big empty ache inside?" I asked. "It's like an explosion inside," he sighed. And I could see he meant it. We were close. I put my arm around him to give him a hug. He touched me back, fearfully at first, but later as if relieved that we could share. What's it like for twelve-year-old Scott? Like an explosion.

Sixty-year-old Julie and family wouldn't celebrate Christmas this year nor any year—at least not without the stabbing pain of separation. Her son was in prison. It wasn't the first year of Christmas without him, but after eleven such Christmases it was not getting any easier. We drank coffee together as she sighed, "You know, they don't just lock him in; they lock us out, too." The words came from the deepest part of her heart, as if they had been imprisoned there. What's it like for sixty-year-old Julie? Like being locked out.

Eighty-two-year-old Hanna sat patiently at the end of the hall. Always pleasant, if a bit incoherent, she caused me to wonder if she really knew where she was. The nursing home staff all praised her, calling her "cute" and "sweet." As we spoke she mentioned visitors coming into "the place," ones who "found out what it was really like and then left." Did she mean the staff or family visitors? Did she mean inspectors? Angels? Demons? "What is it like to be here?"

43

I asked. I was only half looking for an answer since I was uncertain as to her ability to respond. She surprised me. "It's like you've lost something; and you keep looking for it, but you can never find it." Her words chased away any doubts I had had about her coherence. She knew where she was and how she felt. What's it like for eighty-two-year-old Hanna? Like searching and never finding.

Scott's hurt was a hot explosion. Julie's, a helpless caging out. Hanna's, a useless searching. Each different. Each with unique words to describe his or her sacred experience—words that no one could formulate for them. What's it like? What's it like for you? What shape do the events of your life take? How do you share these meanings? To whom can you relate?

Thirty-year-old Jesus chose words to describe his hurt. He reflected on his experience with words that enfold our experience as well: "Truly, truly, I say to you, unless a grain of wheat falls into the earth and dies, it remains alone; but if it dies, it bears much fruit" (John 12:24). What's it like for thirty-year-old Jesus? Like dying and rising.

"Now is my soul troubled. And what shall I say? 'Father, save me from this hour'? No, for this purpose I have come to this hour. Father, glorify thy name." Then a voice came from heaven, "I have glorified it, and I will glorify it again." The crowd standing by heard it and said that it had thundered. Others said, "An angel has spoken to him." Jesus answered, "This voice has come for your sake, not for mine. Now is the judgment of this world, now shall the ruler of this world be cast out; and I, when I am lifted up from the earth, will draw all men to myself." He said this to show by what death he was to die (John 12:27-33).

And to keep me from being too elated by the abundance of revelations, a thorn was given me in the flesh, a messenger of Satan, to harass me, to keep me from being too elated. Three times I besought the Lord about this, that it should leave me; but he said to me, "My grace is sufficient for you, for my power is made perfect in weakness" (2 Corinthians 12:7-9).

Thank you, Lord Jesus, that you know what it is like—what it is like to live, what it is like to suffer, what it is like to die. Be with us in our situation, whatever it may be. Help us to recognize your grace that is sufficient for us. Amen.

The Heart of the Gospel

I carry the gospel deep within. At times it bubbles hotly, as if today were to be the day that the gates would blast open and the gospel would burst forth pure and holy. But the gurgling gospel seeks to flow, as is its nature. For only in flowing is the gospel real. Only in giving is it truth. Only in sharing is it life.

I carry the gospel deep within and wonder how it is to be shared. As if the gospel were a gun to be drawn in defense! Or a part of me I could peel off and share! But You put Your gospel deep within, and I need to share my heart.

So wise You are to make me share myself! You are wise to draw me out, break me forth, let me flow. You burst forth giving life and light, as is Your nature, from the heart of Your gospel Son. No longer is the gospel deep within, but I am in the gospel. And with Your Son I am privileged to share.

On the evening of that day, the first day of the week, the doors being shut where the disciples were, for fear of the Jews, Jesus came and stood among them and said to them, "Peace be with you." When he had said this, he showed them his hands and his side. Then the disciples were glad when they saw the Lord. Jesus said to them again, "Peace be with you. As the Father has sent me, even so I send you." And when he had said this, he breathed on them, and said to them, "Receive the Holy Spirit. If you forgive the sins of any, they are forgiven; if you retain the sins of any, they are retained" (John 20:19-23).

In the year that King Uzziah died I saw the Lord sitting upon a throne, high and lifted up; and his train filled the temple. Above him stood the seraphim; each had six wings: with two he covered his face, and with two he covered his feet, and with two he flew. And one called to another and said:
"Holy, holy, holy is the LORD of hosts;
the whole earth is full of his glory."
And the foundations of the thresholds shook at the voice of him who called, and the house was filled with smoke. And I said: "Woe is me! For I am lost; for I am a man of unclean lips, and I dwell in the midst of a people of unclean lips; for my eyes have seen the King, the LORD of hosts!"

Then flew one of the seraphim to me, having in his hand a burning coal which he had taken with tongs from the altar. And he touched my mouth, and said: "Behold, this has touched your lips; your guilt is taken away, and your sin forgiven." And I heard the voice of the Lord saying, "Whom shall I send, and who will go for us?" Then I said, "Here am I! Send me" (Isaiah 6:1-8).

God, the gospel burns within me. Let its embers glow genuinely, warmly, lovingly. Blow the breath of your Spirit across the coals you have kindled, that your truth and love might burn brightly. When I treat the gospel as a possession or special private treasure, remind me that it is I who sit in your midst and that your gospel fills all, everywhere, with your glory. Amen.

Part 3
Outside In:
Inklings in the World

Life and Death at Work in Us

It was night when the helicopters buzzed into the hospital courtyard. With blades thrashing desperately as if to drive away the darkness, the chopper's characteristic warble cut off the morning's newness. Five doctors and several assistants and nurses emerged from the helicopters. Twins, a boy and a girl, had been born prematurely. The local hospital was not equipped to handle the emergency. Now the mechanical arms of the helicopters became arms of mercy— even of life. As the thrashing became indistinguishable and the whirling blades a faint dot, mother and father, left behind, linked their prayers to the sun's rising. Unspoken hope became loud, heart-felt prayer. It was morning.

The newborn twins were flown directly to an urban hospital where everything possible was done for them. Still, the merciful flight of the helicopters and the best doctors' care were not enough. Less than a day later the little girl died. The boy remained in critical condition.

Now the mother and father's pain is recalled at each helicopter's sight or sound. A chopper becomes to them a symbol of death and separation. Looking skyward at the hint of thrashing blades, they remember their little girl and the morning when darkness remained despite the sun's rising. The helicopter is a constant reminder now, a symbol to recall events too rapidly transpired and too painfully endured to remember any other way. The helicopter stretches the painful experience of loss over the years and helps the too rapid and too deeply cutting experience to be assimilated little by little. The helicopter's gentle hum coaxes acceptance of life and death from suffering. The helicopter becomes God's grace, his vehicle of mercy.

Each of us must surely have such reminders, powerful symbols that carry life's passions that are too abrupt and too powerful for immediate experience. The joys and pains hide in a thousand reminders—an empty beer bottle, a solitary picture on a wall, a ring, a place, a time of year, a gift received or given—only to surface at the appearance of those reminders. A thousand symbols filled with life's meaning call us to God's endless grace and truth; these symbols are given mercifully in memory, lest we be crushed by the heaviness of what they signify.

It was night when the soldiers came. Their crude clubs and hostile torches choked morning's newness before the dark could be dis-

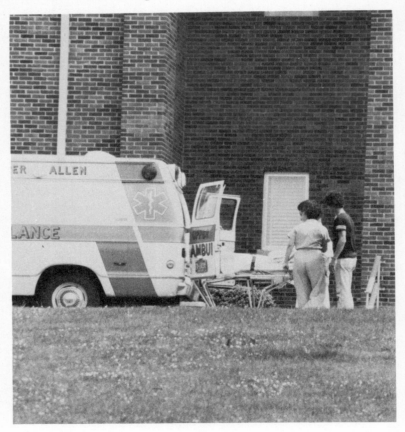

pelled. The weary, pain-filled prayers of the garden gasped hope that the cup might pass. But the thrashing soldiers and the pointing fingers and the loud shouts of "Crucify him! Crucify him!" could already be heard. With cup firmly in hand, Jesus died.

But the cup he bore—too painful, too abrupt, too powerful for our experience—has become the gathering point of all our symbols. In his experience the passion of life was gathered together and turned into the bread of truth and the wine of mercy. God's call to suffering victory is the feast of Easter morning: "Take, eat; this is my body. Do this in remembrance of me. Take, drink; this is my blood. Do this in remembrance of me."

For what we preach is not ourselves, but Jesus Christ as Lord, with ourselves as your servants for Jesus' sake. For it is the God who said, "Let light shine out of darkness," who has shone in our hearts to give the light of the knowledge of the glory of God in the face of Christ.

But we have this treasure in earthen vessels, to show that the transcendent power belongs to God and not to us. We are afflicted in every way, but not crushed; perplexed, but not driven to despair; persecuted, but not forsaken; struck down, but not destroyed; always carrying in the body the death of Jesus, so that the life of Jesus may also be manifested in our bodies. For while we live we are always being given up to death for Jesus' sake, so that the life of Jesus may be manifested in our mortal flesh. So death is at work in us, but life in you (2 Corinthians 4:5-12).

God, I live a life full of reminders—some I cling to happily, others I ardently avoid. Open me to your grace and truth in my memories and experience. Let death and life work wonders in your name. Amen.

Dusty Treasures

A stack of maple offering plates collected dust in Steve's back closet. Originally he had planned to give them to the church; but as he turned them on the lathe, one rim became smaller than the other, and as he sanded, one spot remained rough. The varnish had run a little in one place; and though one could hardly notice these things, the plates just weren't perfect. So Steve had hidden them in his back closet as if the years would somehow make the plates more perfect. Instead, they only collected dust.

We were talking in Steve's living room. I was unloading some frustrations and disappointments, sharing some loneliness, giving voice to some ragged edges I was feeling. I spoke of what a young Jesuit had once shared with me: our communion is a broken one. Our communion is a ragged one—with a sharp point here and a dull edge there; here a tattered face and there a resistant smile. A wrinkle, a mismatch, a tear—our communion is not perfect but broken, as the bread we share is broken. And perhaps it is because of its brokenness and humanness that it is so important, for here God touches us deeply where our strengths and assets cannot get in the way.

Steve excused himself. I thought that perhaps I had completely missed him, boring him with theological drivel. But he returned shortly with four offering plates piled high, saying, "I never brought them out for three years, but now I think I can give them to the church." We saw the one with the narrower rim, and the rough spot on another. We touched the place where the varnish had run. They weren't perfect, but somehow God had made them so—in their offering.

O Lord, open thou my lips,
 and my mouth shall show forth thy praise.
For thou hast no delight in sacrifice;
 were I to give a burnt offering, thou wouldst not be pleased.
The sacrifice acceptable to God is a broken spirit;
 a broken and contrite heart, O God, thou wilt not despise.
 —Psalm 51:15-17

And every priest stands daily at his service, offering repeatedly the same sacrifices, which can never take away sins. But when Christ had offered for all time a single sacrifice for sins, he sat down at the right hand of God, then to wait until his enemies should be made a stool for his feet. For by a single offering he has perfected for all time those who are sanctified. And the Holy Spirit also bears witness to us; for after saying,
"This is the covenant that I will make with them
after those days, says the Lord:
I will put my laws on their hearts,
and write them on their minds,"
then he adds,
"I will remember their sins and their misdeeds no more."
Where there is forgiveness of these, there is no longer any offering for sin (Hebrews 10:11-18).

Jesus, your offering on the cross was perfect, wholly acceptable to God. We live in the joy of your gracious offering. When we seek to be perfect ourselves, remind us that we live in you and need not justify ourselves. When we are reluctant to offer our gifts, both our wholeness and our hurts, inspire us by your example to give joyously. Create in us a clean heart and renew a right spirit within us. Amen.

Basketball Communion

The bouncing basketball sounded lonesome in the half-filled gymnasium. The game was no longer interesting; persistent, emotion-filled yelling wasted away between deaf ears. Mark's mother has cancer. The hospital. Surgery. Radiation. Hopeless.

His face was too tired to conceal the emotion that was too strong to hide. Two weeks she had been there. Hadn't there been a melancholy about Mark? Hadn't he nonverbally communicated a depth of pain? So many things go on in an adolescent's mind: I had thought perhaps a fight with his girlfriend or a bad day at school—but not that his mother was dying. . . .

"Can I do anything?" As I asked, I sensed my own helplessness and weakness, even faithlessness. To speak seemed only an escape; to remain silent, an avoidance. I asked a probing question . . . and Mark talked. Amid the bouncing balls, the ringing bells, and periodic outbursts of applause, there was a corner conversation with the depth of Communion and the shallowness of words. "Can I pray for you?" Already we were praying as the world kept going and the time clock sped towards its running out.

Then Diane was back—sixteen, with popcorn, and sharing her boyfriend's concern. "Without Diane I wouldn't make it." Mark was ministered to. The bouncing goes on—I wonder how the corner conversations, wedged within the confines of noise and activity, still fill the empty spaces between persons. I smile at God for being so prudent as to use so many instruments in all situations.

If one member suffers, all suffer together; if one member is honored, all rejoice together.

Now you are the body of Christ and individually members of it (1 Corinthians 12:26-27).

And they came to Bethsaida. And some people brought to him a blind man, and begged him to touch him. And he took the blind man by the hand, and led him out of the village; and when he had spit on his eyes and laid his hands upon him, he asked him, "Do you see anything?" And he looked up and said, "I see men; but they look like trees, walking." Then again he laid his hands upon his eyes; and he looked intently and was restored, and saw everything clearly. And he sent him away to his home, saying, "Do not even enter the village" (Mark 8:22-26).

Our prayers are often silent ones whispered in the corners of our activities. Make our life prayer. Make our conversation and our reaching and our touching our worship. Make our love our praise of you, God. Amen.

When Evil Breaks In

Sarah and her nine-year-old friend skipped home from school near the military installation where their fathers both worked. Time and again their parents had warned them to stay on the main path and especially to avoid the woods that surrounded the camp. But it was one of those days when spring soothed away all cares and beckoned nothing but hopeful, happy thoughts about the human condition. Along their way they heard the irresistible call of a bird chirping excitedly in the woods. They followed its bidding.

As they wandered, following the frightened twitters, they came across a baby bird that had fallen out of its nest. Two sets of hands reached down in concern and love. Trading off holding their precious finding, they began their trek homeward. Before they could find their way out of the woods, however, they were confronted with an army jeep and three soldiers. "Whatcha got there, little girl?" inquired one of the green-clad men. With springlike innocence Sarah held out their prize: "A little bird who fell out of his nest." "Lemme see it, little girl," he demanded. Placing the bird gently on the ground in front of him, the soldier looked first at his friends and then at the two girls as he raised his armorlike boot and crushed the fledgling into the ground. Sarah's vision blurred in disbelief as the soldiers' faces became those of laughing, green-scaled monsters in front of her. The girls turned and fled, the horrible vision of slaughter hot in their heads.

The story is Sarah's true experience, one recalled only painfully. But the story is ours as well. Who among us has not experienced the hope of spring—that our guard no longer need be up, that we can trust once more, that we can live openly and love again? And who among us has not been burned by human promises broken or set up by sympathy and crushed by outright evil or perhaps just slowly deflated by repeated little setbacks, those times when others have not come through and we've been let down? Who among us has not sensed the capricious injustice of suffering, when the very best of intentions have been thwarted unfairly and the noblest beginnings are hacked off without a chance of fruition? It is not just Sarah who wonders why. It is not just her nine-year-old playmate who questions the meaning of events unimaginable and, yet, not uncommon. It is humanity's heart that aches with unanswerable experience. It is the human spirit made heavy with unfairness. It is humankind's hands that reach out and seem never to join cleanly in compassion. Sarah's experience touches ours wherever injustice and evil confront us. And we ask heart-deep questions.

For one is approved if, mindful of God, he endures pain while suffering unjustly. For what credit is it, if when you do wrong and are beaten for it you take it patiently? But if when you do right and suffer for it you take it patiently, you have God's approval. For to this you have been called, because Christ also suffered for you, leaving you an example, that you should follow in his steps. He committed no sin; no guile was found on his lips. When he was reviled, he did not revile in return; when he suffered, he did not threaten; but he trusted to him who judges justly. He himself bore our sins in his body on the tree, that we might die to sin and live to righteousness. By his wounds you have been healed (1 Peter 2:19-24).

And the soldiers led him away inside the palace (that is, the praetorium); and they called together the whole battalion. And they clothed him in a purple cloak, and plaiting a crown of thorns they put it on him. And they began to salute him, "Hail, King of the Jews!" And they struck his head with a reed, and spat upon him, and they knelt down in homage to him. And when they had mocked him, they stripped him of the purple cloak, and put his own clothes on him. And they led him out to crucify him (Mark 15:16-20).

God, when we are broken by disappointment, crushed by injustice, when our hopes for humanity are shattered before our eyes, open your arms to us. Let the arms of the cross enfold us and the power of your resurrection assure us. Amen.

A Time for Flying

The little owls return nightly between 8:50 and 9:05. It wasn't that long ago that their furry little bodies found refuge behind forester Graham's home. Both Mr. and Mrs. Graham have a gift for animals—especially birds. Together they have nursed numerous sea gulls, robins, pelicans, and now these owls back to health and the wilds. Now the little owls return for nightly visits to feast on hamburger or to perch on Mrs. Graham's shoulder or to peck playfully at loving fingers. It won't be long until they will be completely on their own, hunting their own food and forgetting the generosity of their human caretakers. For the owls it will be time to be themselves completely.

The Graham children have a curfew, too, which has been agreed upon mutually. Past ten o'clock is too late; though it is usually ten or a few minutes after, and only rarely before, that finds the children returning to the door. It wasn't too long before that, that their little feet had thumped from room to room and their laughing and crying had filled the house with life. Soon they will be on their own, in their own houses, sharing their laughter and tears with other young faces. Will they forget the loving generosity of faithful parents? Will they leave the comfortable nest without the least acknowledgment of gratitude? They will leave and become themselves—and they'll become caretakers of wild ones and children. They'll know the love and heartache of giving self. They'll see God more clearly. The time will come.

We are children stretching our wings, returning weekly or daily to be fed by the bread of life. Playfully or tearfully we offer our praise while God cares continually, watching the horizon anxiously

for our fluttering movement of return. God's arms are full of love for us. The Caretaker who makes us fly makes us fully ourselves. Both little owls and children God loves.

> Blessed be the LORD,
>   who has not given us
>   as prey to their teeth!
> We have escaped as a bird
>   from the snare of the fowlers;
> the snare is broken,
>   and we have escaped!
>
> Our help is in the name of the LORD,
>   who made heaven and earth.
>   —Psalm 124:6-8

"Therefore I tell you, do not be anxious about your life, what you shall eat or what you shall drink, nor about your body, what you shall put on. Is not life more than food, and the body more than clothing? Look at the birds of the air: they neither sow nor reap nor gather into barns, and yet your heavenly Father feeds them. Are you not of more value than they? And which of you by being anxious can add one cubit to his span of life? And why are you anxious about clothing? Consider the lilies of the field, how they grow; they neither toil nor spin; yet I tell you, even Solomon in all his glory was not arrayed like one of these. But if God so clothes the grass of the field, which today is alive and tomorrow is thrown into the oven, will he not much more clothe you, O men of little faith? Therefore do not be anxious, saying, 'What shall we eat?' or 'What shall we drink?' or 'What shall we wear?' For the Gentiles seek all these things; and your heavenly Father knows that you need them all. But seek first his kingdom and his righteousness, and all these things shall be yours as well.

"Therefore do not be anxious about tomorrow, for tomorrow will be anxious for itself. Let the day's own trouble be sufficient for the day" (Matthew 6:25-34).

And his gifts were that some should be apostles, some prophets, some evangelists, some pastors and teachers, to equip the saints for the work of ministry, for building up the body of Christ, until we all attain to the unity of the faith and of the knowledge of the Son of God, to mature manhood, to the measure of the stature of the fulness of Christ; so that we may no longer be children, tossed to and fro and carried about with every wind of doctrine, by the cunning of men, by their craftiness in deceitful wiles. Rather, speaking the truth in love, we are to grow up in every way into him who is the head, into Christ, from whom the whole body, joined and knit together by every joint with which it is supplied, when each part is working properly, makes bodily growth and upbuilds itself in love (Ephesians 4:11-16).

Thank you, Source of Life, for the gift of family. Thank you, Fountain of Love, for the gift of friendship. Thank you, Spirit of Truth, for the gift of community. Help us to be generous as parents, gracious as children, and loving as your people. Amen.

Remember Me?

The truth leapt unfalteringly from her stress-flattened lips: "You can't even pay someone to remember your name." The divorce had dragged on unnecessarily. All was in order—at least to the extent that separation can be orderly—yet the finalization eluded capture. The day came. Full of anticipation that finally things would be settled, that she would no longer be up in the air about who owned what or who she was or what she could or could not do, that finally the divorce would be over, she waited impatiently in the courtroom. The moment so crushingly important arrived. But her lawyer didn't show. The whole procedure had to be postponed. The divorce was not over. The needed attorney failed to make his appearance.

To be sure, it was probably an oversight, a mistake the terrible consequences of which were not understood. Or perhaps time for him was of a different order, neatly sectioned into blocks and appointments. Perhaps the spaces in his book had no names, only cold, digital hours and scribbled places; no faces, only clear case numbers; no life, only illegible notes written hastily in the margins.

Now the truth leapt from her heart: "You can't even pay someone to remember your name." The truth gathered momentum as it tumbled from her tongue, as if it had been conceived long before and only now had come to birth. Not yet mature, newborn, the truth bounced innocently between us, pointing beyond itself to its creator.

I, too, search desperately for a name, for my being in relation to others. How do I fit in? What do I contribute to the whole? Who am

PREACH THE GOSPEL

HOLY BIBLE

IN MEMORIAM·
REV JOHN P WALTER· BORN 1810 DIED 1864·
THE FIRST LICENTIATE OF THIS CHURCH·

I? Where am I loved and needed? I, too, cannot buy remembrance—I can't purchase an unexpected birthday card or surprise visit. I can't coerce a concerned telephone call or cheery hello. I can't buy self-respect or friendship or love.

But I am given a name, a place, a value. I am given remembrance in One who died for me. I am known, and therefore I know. My name is a child of the One who never forgets. The truth of the need for a name stands face-to-face with the truth of the Name-giver. Not bought or sold, bargained or cajoled. But given.

". . . the sheep hear his voice, and he calls his own sheep by name and leads them out. . . . I am the good shepherd; I know my own and my own know me, as the Father knows me and I know the Father; and I lay down my life for the sheep" (John 10:3, 14-15).

For I received from the Lord what I also delivered to you, that the Lord Jesus on the night when he was betrayed took bread, and when he had given thanks, he broke it, and said, "This is my body which is for you. Do this in remembrance of me." In the same way also the cup, after supper, saying, "This cup is the new covenant in my blood. Do this, as often as you drink it, in remembrance of me." For as often as you eat this bread and drink the cup, you proclaim the Lord's death until he comes (1 Corinthians 11:23-26).

In the name of God, our Creator, Redeemer, and Sanctifier. Amen. We would live in your name. We would receive our identity from you. We would be remembered into being by you. Thank you for remembering us even to death. Amen.